The Collection of Emotions

Tina Namiranian

BookLeaf Publishing

India | USA | UK

Presentation by *BookLeaf Publishing*

Web: www.bookleafpub.com

E-mail: info@bookleafpub.com

ISBN: 9789358311860

First edition 2023

This is dedicated towards all the people in my life who have ever encouraged me to keep going.

ACKNOWLEDGEMENT

I would like to thank and acknowledge my greatest teacher in writing as of now, who has greatly changed my perspective on the pure topic and idea of literature, Ms. La Monica Bryson. Throughout the entirety of my eighth grade year, I felt overwhelmed with the workload and the general ideas that she presented us with and expected for us to grow on. However, I am eternally grateful for all of the knowledge that she has passed down upon me since it has really inspired me to write more and gain this aspiration to become a future writer. Of course, I would also like to thank my other English teacher as well, Ms. Alison Schulman, who was able to work with me one on one and help me with my weaknesses. She was able to magnificently teach us even through a tough online year, and I very much appreciate her efforts. Lastly, I would like to thank all my friends and family, for their encouragement and for simply believing in me. I wouldn't be here without them. Specifically, I would like to thank my best friend, Emma Vicenico. She and I met a long time ago, or so it feels like, through a swim team. We have become close every since and she is my second reason for writing these poems.

My first, would have to be my parents. Thank you Mom and Dad for believing in me every step of the way and pushing me to be in uncomfortable situations so that I am able to learn and become comfortable in the most difficult times. Thanks for always trying to give me the best opportunities, even when those same opportunities weren't provided for you. Thanks for making me, me.

Happy

Sun, Shining
Sunscreen, Melting
Summer, Ablazing
Love, Pool
Fast, Swim
Water, Cool
Sweet, Watermelon
Funny, Friends
Swaggy, Shades
Almost, Over
School, Comes
Yet, Again
Pack, Work
Teachers, Trying
Students, Cry
Parents, Ablazing
When, Bored
Sun, Shines
Me, Play
Until, Moonrise
During, School
Always, Recall
Summer, Fun
Coming, Wait
When, Comes
Beach, Ball

Anger

2

Hate, Love
Evil, Innocence
Purposeful, Accident
Never, Same
Life, Death
Car, Crash
Sound, RING
Blood, Bath
Devil, Angel
Innocence, Evil
Love, Hate
Person, Devil

Satisfaction

When the food marches down to the depths
filled with acid,
I am satisfied.
When I score a bucket after endless hours of
practice,
I am satisfied.
When the news reports protests in a multitude of
countries for basic rights such as the simple
choice of choosing to show our hair, yet after all
the fight, all is as it was.
I am not satisfied.
When consciously making decisions everyday to
hurt others out of self-hatred.
I am not satisfied.
When making efforts to respect others freedoms
and emotions.
I will be satisfied.

Loneliness

Like a puppy in a pound I lie there
Whimpering alone, trapped in my cage
Watching my hopes and aspirations of what
I hoped to be
Die

Watching friends and family leave
While I sit here on this cold concrete floor
Waiting anxiously for someone to choose me
Love me.

But in the end
It is what it is
People aren't fair
Life is not fair.

So there I stay
Longing for any home
With no one beside me
Besides my barfed on, chew toy.

Appreciation

Blessed, am I to be here today.
Watering and mowing, down my lawn
Burning amongst the sun, the star of our
universe.
To be here listening to the soft whistle of the
breeze tickling my ear
Eating many brussel sprouts, green and stinky, to
maintain my health
This life of labor may not be as we please, but
having this capability,
Is the greatest blessing of all.

Desperation

Oh, so high is the sky I wish to fly
So high are those above that I know it must
And has to be better up there
Than here near the dirty ground
Infested with weeds and bickering mouths

But up there it's different
Serene and blue
If Rapunzel got out of her tower
I can too

All I'm asking is to be
Exactly like them
Make me great
Help me live

Up in that beautiful sky
Oh, I'll do whatever I must,
even if I have to die.

Get me up there.

Excitement

AAA!
It's finally here,
After all those long and painful, treacherous
years,
I wouldn't go back, without a doubt
These couple years have been a terrible
roundabout

At least in these years, a couple things kept me
going,
My friends, cold coffee, and
Of course today,
Where everything is finally easygoing.

My new favorite letters, G, then R, A, and D.
All spell what I have forever been waiting for,
My graduation day!

Numb

As thick as a stump
 As strong as the wind
  I feel nothing
   Not even a prick
    Stuck I am with no one here to help
     Only those who push me constantly
      To go prick my finger on that spinning
wheel.
        I try to not listen, I really do,
         But after all this pushing
          I feel as if I do.
           Death watches as I follow along
            Play my part as it sings along
            And when the play ends
            My life stayed as it is
             Invisible and Meaningless
             Besides having Mr. Death take me in.

Joy

The bright colors, the bows, the shine,
Oh, how they just call out my name
Whispering to me
Ever so quietly,
Open me, I'm quite
Big!
The sparkle it brings to me
That one person ever so gratefully
Gave me this treasure out of the pureness in their
soul
For their joy
Gave me joy
And now we both laugh along.

Sadness

I'm as dead as I am alive, drifting with no
purpose,
I feel as if I've cried out my soul on purely
today's short notice.
With one simple mistake, itty-bitty and small, I
have wiped out my existence
If it wasn't already erased at all.
What I shouldn't have said, done, and thought is
all over now,
Thanks to my "best friend" who had to blurt it
all out.
Is it my fault?
I rather not decide, whether it's me, her, or them,
I'm still about to cry.

Calm

The breeze sways across my bedroom,
Waking me from my slumber,
Luring me to slither out of bed and enjoy a little
outside-time.
I listen to its calling steady and strong,
Waiting ever so quietly hoping I can play along.
I wish I were the breeze, so swift yet so calm,
Helping others quietly, helping them sing along.

Anxiety

Hours,
Minutes,
Seconds,
Oh, who am I kidding,
I'm already late!
Late to my class, my job, my wedding,
But, right now I just can't think, I can't stop sweating
Too fast, too soon, why is it running?
The time, too fast, I can't keep on chasing.
I'm running out of breath, I can't, keep talking,
I think this is the end, not now, not already
No, go away, I just need a bit more time.
I need to win this race
AH, WAIT, I FORGOT!
I'll be back in five.

Hope

For what is succession without failure,
Winning without losing,
One needs the other or else both will be
unmoving.
A team can't win without an opponent,
A track star can't place first without a second,
This relationship will tear you down
Squish every fiber of your existence to pieces,
But, then it is because of that relationship you
are then able to rise,
Higher than no one has before,
Since the more you are beaten up
The higher you are able to soar.
What was once a seed
Can only sprout after years and years
Of thunderous weather,
Then finally it can begin its route.

Dread

Summer shuts her doors, leaving us cold to the
bone
The nightmares of the past leave the shore and
come to haunt
All those failed grades weren't even as close to
the
Scary looks of failure upon those we love.
The more failure I gain the more permanent my
failed future has become.
I'm sick of this failure; I'm all maxed out.
School please go away,
I can do without.

Interest

My favorite topic is new,
Everything about it is just fresh and organic.
Nothing is wasted, nothing reused
You explore and implore these new endless
views.
A new puzzle you say, will give me the
challenge
There surely isn't a problem I can't manage,
And even if I can't
Whatevs, no big deal,
I'll just ask for some help,
At the end of the day,
Im learning
Help or no help.

Confusion

Its knotted, these laces of my mind,
Braiding into every nerve in my body,
keeping me alive.
As I sit surrounded by those with,
bow-tied brains.
Mine can't seem to match the screen,
No matter what's at stake.
I can't take this humiliation,
Why isn't it clear?
What made this fog come,
while there's disappeared?
Dumb
   Stupid
      Idiot
I can't
Cut it loose already, I give up.

Awe

Off the roof,
No way,
Never in a billion years
Dang, what a shocker

#livingontheedge

That's what I live for,
Did you see that
Those moments,
Moments where in that one place
At the one time
I feel peace and wonder for a second at a time.
How hard is it to take one moment,
One second out of your day,
Everyday, and do something you would never do
So that tomorrow you can say
I did something new.

Boredom

Over
And Over,
And Over,
And Over,
Wake up,
Eat
Sleep
And good morning
That's my daily routine,
And until the end of my days that's all it will be
For what is there in life that can make me feel
free,
This awful place I'm trapped in,
Can't wait for my new beginning
Since everything is so dull here
I wish for it all to be shiny
Finally, some change
Maybe even some
Fun
One word
Three letters
One lifetime
Now just begun.

Admiration

The twinkle and glitter rushing past me as a
human figure sprints across
Leaving only her spark and Chanel No.5 scent
behind for us to scrap upon
Stunning I say, so stunning the stars are jealous

When she's not sprinting past, she is sprinting
out on the court,
With her perfect hair flicking as she scores,
scores, and scores.
She never sweats, oh no, she would never,
She just keeps shining bright, until she is the
winner.

To be her would be such a wonder,
Thankfully, all I have to do
Is just keep working harder.

Jealousy

Golden locks of luscious gold call my name,
The ocean trapped behind glass spheres,
Hills of pink flowers filled with the purest
sunshine,
Plump and shiny roads.
My Dream

When I awake,
Muddy, matted rags surround me,
Spheres filled with dirt and spit,
As the hills turn to sand dunes with sinking
holes,
The shiny roads now broken, cracked from all
the damage they've taken.
My Nightmare, now reality.

Life

(l•l•E•f)

You have one shot,
One
That's it.

That's way less than the number of times I
wanted to quit.
These feelings, emotions you have bottled up in
inside
I feel you and them,
It's alright, you'll be fine.

We weren't meant to be perfect,
Always succeed, never fail
That lifestyle is hard anyways,
Mistakes are very real.

There is no real way your life should be lived,
No guidebook, no teacher, and definitely no
friend
To tell you how to live your life,
So you don't regret it
In the End.

You make your life,
Your way, at your time,
It's all up to you when you say
Goodbye.

Just know one thing,
A small detail perhaps,
These emotions are real
So be gentle, relax.

You will be okay.

With every good, there is always bad,
Like there is a sun for the moon,
It makes things balanced,
Simple and smooth.

You might not love the way that it works,
Having to feel lonely, and sad until it begins to
work,
But that's just how it is,
Some might even say it's a blessing,
For it shows you a path to a better,

                                        brighter,

                                              new

ending.

Don't follow a path,
Create your own.

www.ingramcontent.com/pod-product-compliance
Lightning Source LLC
LaVergne TN
LVHW051250200726
843510LV00011B/1786